Lerner SPORTS™

SPORTS VIPs

MEET CHLOE KIM

MARGARET J. GOLDSTEIN

Lerner Publications ◆ Minneapolis

Lerner Publications Company
An imprint of Lerner Publishing Group, Inc.
241 First Avenue North
Minneapolis, MN 55401 USA

For reading levels and more information, look up this title at www.lernerbooks.com.

Main body text set in Aptifer Slab LT Pro. Typeface provided by Linotype AG.

Library of Congress Cataloging-in-Publication Data

Names: Goldstein, Margaret J., author.
Title: Meet Chloe Kim / Margaret J. Goldstein.
Description: Minneapolis, MN : Lerner Publications, [2023] | Series: Sports VIPs (Lerner Sports) | Includes bibliographical references and index. | Audience: Ages 7–11 years | Audience: Grades 4–6 | Summary: "Snowboarder Chloe Kim became a fan favorite at the 2018 Winter Olympics when she won gold on the halfpipe. She followed it up with another gold medal in 2022. Read about her life and career"— Provided by publisher.
Identifiers: LCCN 2022019980 (print) | LCCN 2022019981 (ebook) | ISBN 9781728476001 (Library Binding) | ISBN 9781728478609 (Paperback) | ISBN 9781728484907 (eBook)
Subjects: LCSH: Kim, Chloe, 2000-—Juvenile literature. | Snowboarders—United States—Biography—Juvenile literature. | Snowboarding—Juvenile literature. | Asian American athletes—United States—Biography—Juvenile literature. | Women Olympic athletes—United States—Biography—Juvenile literature.
Classification: LCC GV857.S57 G67 2023 (print) | LCC GV857.S57 (ebook) | DDC 796.939092 [B]—dc23/eng/20220509

LC record available at https://lccn.loc.gov/2022019980
LC ebook record available at https://lccn.loc.gov/2022019981

Manufactured in the United States of America
1-52168-50630-8/4/2022

TABLE OF CONTENTS

TRIPLE PLAY

Chloe Kim was having a great day. She had the lead in the women's halfpipe contest at the 2016 US Snowboarding Grand Prix. On her first run, she'd earned a sky-high score of 96.5 out of a possible 100. She was back for her third and final run. Could she score even higher this time?

She began with a method grab. Next, she soared high in the air, spinning around once . . . twice . . . three times. Spinning three times, a move called a 1080, was difficult. But no one was surprised to see Kim do it well. After all, she was one of the best snowboarders in the world.

FAST FACTS

DATE OF BIRTH: April 23, 2000
EVENT: Halfpipe
TEAM: US Snowboard Team

PROFESSIONAL HIGHLIGHTS: two Olympic gold medals; two World Championship gold medals; six Winter X Games gold medals; two Winter Youth Olympics gold medals

PERSONAL HIGHLIGHTS: lived in Switzerland for two years; studied at Princeton University; speaks English, Korean, and French; appeared on the TV show *The Masked Singer*; likes to play guitar and ride horses

Kim soars during one of her halfpipe runs in the 2016 US Snowboarding Grand Prix.

What happened next *was* a surprise. Right after the 1080, Kim did the same trick again. This time she spun in the opposite direction. No woman had ever done back-to-back 1080s in competition. The crowd clapped and whooped. The event announcer said, "Ladies and gentleman, you have just witnessed history!"

When Kim ended her run, the other competitors rushed over to congratulate her. She waved to the crowd and laughed with joy. She celebrated even more when she saw the scoreboard. She had earned a perfect score: 100 points.

This was remarkable. In the history of halfpipe competition, only one other boarder had ever scored 100. That was Shaun White, an Olympic gold medalist. Chloe Kim joined him in the record books.

But when it came to snowboarding records, she was just getting started. She was only 15 years old. Even bigger things were in store.

Kim (*left*) celebrates with snowboarding legend Kelly Clark after Kim's perfect score of 100 at the 2016 US Snowboarding Grand Prix.

CHAPTER 1

ON BOARD

Chloe Kim was born on April 23, 2000, in Long Beach, California, a community near Los Angeles. She started snowboarding early. Her dad, Jong Jin Kim, wanted to learn the sport himself. On weekends, he drove to Mountain High Ski Resort in the San Gabriel Mountains near Los Angeles. He took four-year-old Chloe with him. They both took snowboarding lessons.

Chloe was a natural on a snowboard. She learned to do turns, 180s, and ollies. At the age of six, she joined the Mountain High Snowboard Team. With this group, she competed against other girls her age.

Kim, shown here at the age of 13, quickly became one of snowboarding's rising stars.

SUPER SPORTS SCOOP

At snowboarding competitions, a panel of judges rates each run on a scale of 0 to 100. Riders earn high scores by nailing difficult and new tricks, multiple flips and spins, board grabs, and high jumps. Judges also compare competitors to one another to determine who deserves the higher score.

Chloe's parents had immigrated to the United States from South Korea. Nearly every year, the family traveled to South Korea to see relatives. Chloe learned to speak Korean from her parents and other family members. Her parents also wanted her to learn French. So they sent her to live with an aunt in Geneva, Switzerland, where French is one of the main languages. Chloe spent third and fourth grade in Geneva. There, she not only learned French but also snowboarded in the Swiss Alps.

CHAPTER 2

AIRBORNE

When Chloe returned to the United States, she took her sport to the next level. On weekends, she and her dad drove six hours from Los Angeles to Mammoth Mountain in eastern California. This area had top-level snowboarding facilities.

Chloe joined the Mammoth Mountain Snowboard Team when she was 10 years old. She competed in halfpipe and superpipe events. She soared high above the lip of the snow-covered pipe, performing spins, grabs, and airs. In slopestyle contests, she slid down metal rails and shot over jumps, performing tricks along the way.

Kim pulls off a trick at Mammoth Mountain Resort in 2014.

Olympic snowboarding coach Mike Jankowski was among the teachers who helped Kim develop her skills.

Chloe won competition after competition. The snowboarding world took notice. In 2013, she was named to the US Snowboarding Team. She competed against the best boarders in the world—and she won. "She's a special one," said Olympic snowboarding coach Mike Jankowski. "I've never seen anyone like her."

Thirteen-year-old Kim performs a grab at the 2014 US Snowboarding Grand Prix.

Chloe's high scores with the US team qualified her to compete at the 2014 Winter Olympics. But the International Ski Federation had set the minimum age for Olympians at 15. Chloe was just 13, so she couldn't join the team.

She did compete at the 2016 Winter Youth Olympics in Lillehammer, Norway. She won two gold medals there, in halfpipe and slopestyle. She continued to win big at the Winter X Games, the US Snowboarding Grand Prix, and other contests.

SUPER SPORTS SCOOP

At the 2016 Winter Youth Olympics, organizers chose Chloe to carry the US flag at the opening ceremony. "The Youth Olympic Games are a once-in-a-lifetime opportunity, and it's a really cool moment to be selected as flag bearer for Team USA," she said. "Being able to represent a sport I'm so passionate about is a great honor."

Training, practicing, and traveling to competitions took a tremendous amount of time. It was hard for Chloe to attend school regularly. Mammoth High School, in the town where she trained, hosted a program for student athletes like Chloe. She didn't have to go to class in person. Instead, she did her schoolwork at ski areas around the world, anywhere she happened to be competing. She sent in her homework and communicated with her teachers online.

Kim poses with her gold medal at the 2016 Winter Youth Olympics in Norway.

Kim soars through the air during her final run at the 2018 Winter Olympics. She went on to win the gold medal in the halfpipe.

When the 2018 Olympic Games rolled around, Chloe was old enough and ready to ride. The Games took place in South Korea, her parents' homeland. Some of her Korean relatives traveled to the Olympic host city of Pyeongchang to watch her ride. She did not disappoint them or her other fans. She competed in the halfpipe, where she again landed back-to-back 1080s. Her score of 98.25 gave her the gold medal.

CHAPTER 3

IN THE SPOTLIGHT

Winning an Olympic gold medal brought Kim great fame. Her picture appeared on magazine covers and Kellogg's Corn Flakes boxes. She gave interviews on TV talk shows. The pop band Maroon 5 made a music video for their song *Girls Like You*. It included clips of famous female athletes and entertainers. Chloe Kim was one of them. Mattel, a toy company, produced a line of Barbie dolls modeled after famous female scientists, athletes, artists, and other heroes. Kim was in that lineup too.

All the attention was stressful for Kim. Everywhere she went, people asked her for selfies and autographs. Some fans even tried to follow her home.

Kim appears on *The Late Late Show with James Corden* in 2018. Chef Gordon Ramsay (*right*) joins the conversation.

SUPER SPORTS SCOOP

In 2020, Kim competed on season four of the TV show *The Masked Singer*. In the show, celebrities hide their real identities and sing for judges. She made it to the semifinals and impressed the judges with her stunning singing voice.

In early 2019, Kim broke her ankle at a competition in Colorado. To let the ankle heal, and also to escape the media spotlight, she decided to take time away from snowboarding. She enrolled at Princeton University in New Jersey.

Many Princeton students knew that Kim was a famous snowboarder. Some of them acted starstruck around her. But others didn't follow snowboarding. They treated her like any other classmate. She focused on anthropology, the study of human cultures.

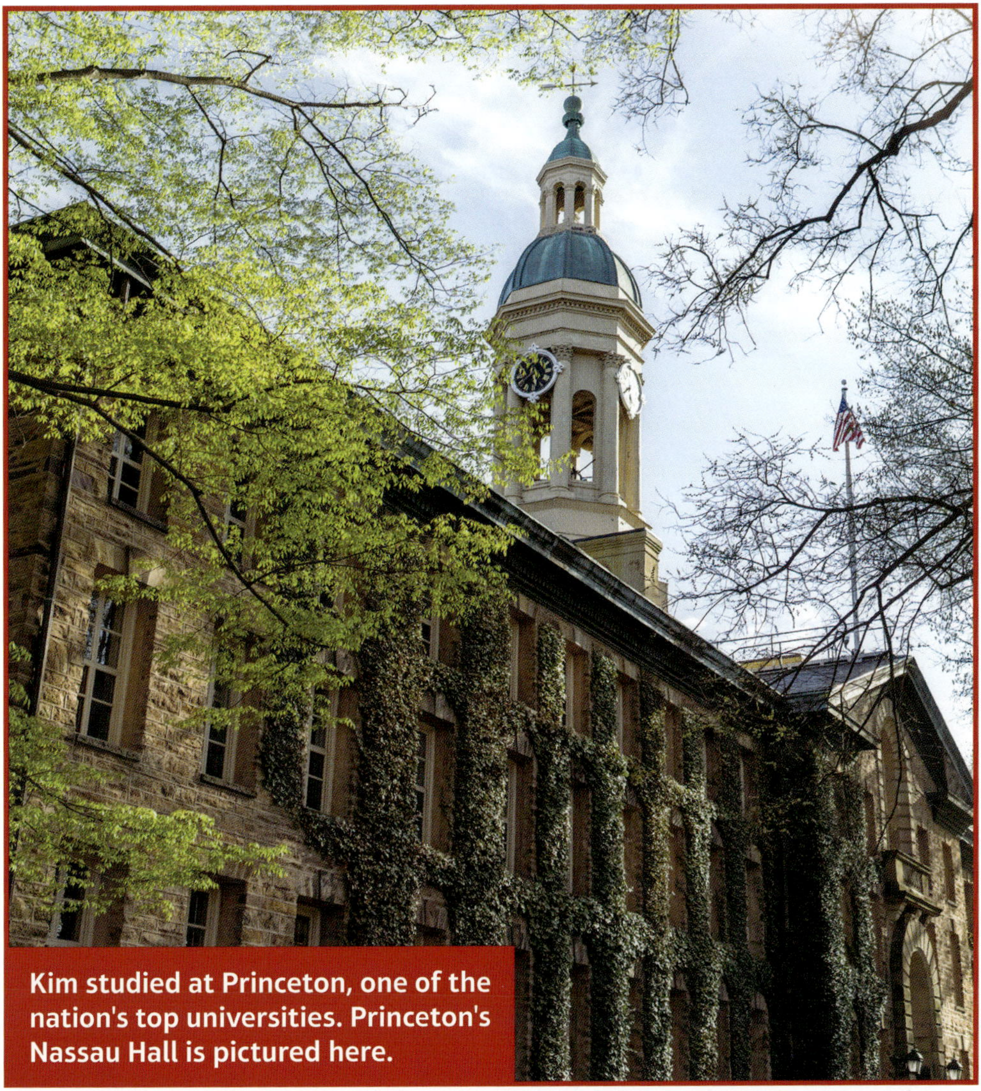

Kim studied at Princeton, one of the nation's top universities. Princeton's Nassau Hall is pictured here.

CHAPTER 4

FLYING HIGH

After 22 months off and studies at Princeton, Kim returned to snowboarding in 2021. She continued her winning ways. She won at the Winter X Games, the World Championships, and other contests. In 2022, she was back on the US Olympic Snowboarding Team.

At the 2022 Olympic Winter Games in Beijing, China, the pressure was on. Everyone expected Kim to win another gold medal in the women's halfpipe. She sailed through the first round. But she needed a big finish to secure the gold. On her first of three final runs, she threw down a stellar series of tricks. The judges liked what they saw. They awarded her a 94 for that run.

Kim begins one of her halfpipe runs at the 2022 Winter Olympics.

Kim shows off her gold medal from the 2022 Winter Olympic halfpipe event.

Kim tried to outdo herself on the second and third runs. Both times she went for a 1260—a spin of three and a half rotations. Both times she fell. It didn't matter. No other competitor could top that 94. The gold medal was hers.

What's next for Chloe Kim? For one thing, she wants to learn new tricks. "I'm constantly trying to push and progress the sport and also push myself," she told a reporter after her Olympic victory. "When I learn a new trick and I do it in a competition . . . that's exciting for me; that's what keeps me going."

SUPER SPORTS SCOOP

Some snowboarding events award prize money to the winners. Top snowboarders also earn money with sponsorships. They appear in advertisements, use gear, and wear clothing showing the sponsor's logo. Kim has had sponsorship deals with the Burton and Roxy snowboard companies, the carmaker Toyota, and many other businesses.

She says she is more at peace with fame than she was after the 2018 Winter Olympics. She better understands how to handle attention from fans and the media, and how not to let it bother her. Although she looks forward to future snowboarding contests, she also treasures her time off the slopes. She likes to hike, skateboard, ride horseback, and play guitar. She also spends time with her dog, an Australian shepherd named Reese, and her boyfriend, former pro skateboarder Evan Berle.

Kim makes a surprise appearance at a restaurant in February 2018 to sign autographs for fans.

Kim grabs the front of her board as she soars through the air at the 2022 Winter Olympics.

The next Winter Olympics is scheduled for Italy in 2026. Will Chloe Kim be there? If she is, one thing is certain: she'll be flying high and taking risks. And there's a good chance she'll be taking home gold.

CHLOE KIM CAREER STATS

HIGHEST HALFPIPE SCORE:

100

OLYMPIC GOLD MEDALS:

2

WORLD CHAMPIONSHIP GOLD MEDALS:

2

WINTER X GAMES GOLD MEDALS:

6

WINTER YOUTH OLYMPICS GOLD MEDALS:

2

GLOSSARY

air: any trick in which a snowboarder is flying through the air

halfpipe: an event in which snowboarders ride through a big U-shaped, snow-covered channel, soar above its walls, and do tricks in the air

immigrate: to move to a new country

method grab: an air that includes grabbing the center of the board with one hand behind the back, with knees bent and the other hand reaching for the sky

ollie: a trick in which a snowboarder puts weight on the tail of the board to pop their body into the air

180: a turn of 180 degrees (half a full spin) carried out while either riding down a slope or in the air

slopestyle: a downhill event in which snowboarders perform tricks on rails and jumps

sponsorship: a business deal in which an athlete agrees to promote a company's products in exchange for money

superpipe: an event that takes place in a halfpipe with walls of 18 feet (5.5 m) or higher

SOURCE NOTES

6 "Chloe Kim's Historic Perfect Score—US Snowboarding Grand Prix 2016," U.S. Ski & Snowboard, February 6, 2016, https://www.youtube.com/watch?v=BjJlFpwhERM&t=69s.

13 John Branch, "Among the Best, but Having to Wait," *New York Times*, January 14, 2014, https://www.nytimes.com/2014/01/19/sports/amid-giggles-a-snowboarding-wizard.html?searchResultPosition=3.

15 "Kim USA Flag Bearer for Youth Olympics," U.S. Ski & Snowboard, February 12, 2016, https://usskiandsnowboard.org/news/kim-usa-flag-bearer-youth-olympics.

25 Michelle Bruton, "Chloe Kim in Much Better Headspace after Winning Second Olympic Gold Medal Than in 2018," *Forbes*, February 21, 2022, https://www.forbes.com/sites/michellebruton/2022/02/21/chloe-kim-in-much-better-headspace-after-winning-second-olympic-gold-medal-than-in-2018/?sh=3e0793bf587c.

LEARN MORE

Allan, John. *Snowboarding*. Minneapolis: Hungry Tomato, 2022.

Extreme Sports Facts
https://www.sciencekids.co.nz/sciencefacts/sports/extremesports.html

Kenney, Karen Latchana. *Extreme Snowboarding Challenges*. Minneapolis: Lerner Publications, 2021.

Scarbrough, Mary Hertz. *Chloe Kim*. Deltaville, VA: High Tide, 2020.

Snowboarding Facts for Kids
https://www.sportsrec.com/9620504/snowboarding-facts-for-kids

This Is Chloe: Read the Story of Chloe Kim
https://www.timeforkids.com/g56/this-is-chloe-kim

INDEX

PHOTO ACKNOWLEDGMENTS

Image credits: AP Photo/Francisco Seco, p. 4; Tom Pennington/Getty Images, pp. 6, 7; Doug Pensinger/Getty Images, pp. 8, 9, 11, 13; Harry How/Getty Images, p. 12; Ezra Shaw/Getty Images, p. 14; Jon Buckle/IOC/Getty Images, p. 16; MARTIN BUREAU/AFP/Getty Images, p. 17; LOIC VENANCE/AFP/Getty Images, p. 18; Terence Patrick/CBS/Getty Images, p. 19; ssguy/Shutterstock, p. 21; Sean M. Haffey/Getty Images, p. 22; Wu Zhuang/Xinhua/Getty Images, p. 23; Maddie Meyer/Getty Images, p. 24; Brittany Murray/MediaNews Group/Long Beach Press-Telegram/Getty Images, p. 26; Kyodo News/Getty Images, p. 27.

Cover image: YUTAKA/AFLO SPORT/Alamy Stock Photo.